MERCEDES-BENZ

Perfection in Luxury and Engineering

Paul W. Cockerham

TODTRI

This book was designed and produced by
TODTRI Book Publishers
P.O. Box 572, New York, NY 10116-0572
FAX: (212) 695-6984

Printed and bound in China

ISBN 1-57717-084-9

Author: Paul W. Cockerham

Publisher: Robert M. Tod
Editor: Edward Douglas
Assistant Editor: Don Kennison
Designer: Mark Weinberg
Typesetting: Command-O Design

Photo Credits

RON KIMBALL
8–9, 17, 43, 44, 45, 50, 58, 63, 64, 65 (top & bottom), 67 (bottom), 70, 71 (top), 77 (top), 78, 79

JOHN LAMM
12, 13, 18 (top & bottom), 20, 21 (top & bottom), 23 (top & bottom),
24–25, 35 (top), 37, 39, 40–41, 48, 56–57, 66, 67 (top), 68 (top & bottom),
69, 71 (bottom), 72–73, 74, 75 (top & bottom), 76, 77 (bottom)

MERCEDES-BENZ
49 (top, bottom right & bottom left), 51 (top & bottom), 52 (top & bottom), 54 (bottom), 59 (top), 60 (top), 62

DENIS L. TANNEY
16 (top & bottom), 28 (top & bottom), 29, 42 (top & bottom)

NICKY WRIGHT
4–5, 6, 10, 11, 14, 15, 19, 22, 26, 27, 30 (top & bottom), 31, 32, 34, 35 (bottom),
36 (top & bottom), 38, 46, 47, 53, 54 (top), 55, 59 (bottom), 60 (bottom), 61

Contents

Introduction

No brand of mass-produced motorcars is more identified with luxury and quality than is that of Mercedes-Benz. Impeccably constructed, the sedans, coupes, and convertibles that bear the three-pointed star reinforce an image of achievement for proven and would-be captains of industry and government worldwide.

Less appreciated is the fact that each Mercedes-Benz retains, to varying degrees, elements of a sporting character. This character springs from a racing history that has known spectacular success, but has only been sporadically pursued by the factory, for reasons both political and tragic. Generally speaking, the legacy of performance that is legitimately Mercedes-Benz's is thus less important to the customer than the traits of image, luxury, reliability, and refinement most attributed to the marque.

Still, the performance is there. Even the underpowered diesel-engined offerings from Daimler-Benz A.G. provide sprightly handling characteristics. And the stoic executive cruisers that are Mercedes-Benz's flagship creations are so capacitated that they can stealthily rocket along the autobahn in excess of 150 miles per hour (240 kilometers per hour), their passengers coddled in luxury and near silence.

This volume is a subjective catalog of those Mercedes-Benz automobiles that have, over the company's 110-plus-year history, inspired excitement in driving enthusiasts.

Such enthusiasts have been rewarded from the company's earliest days. Both Gottlieb Daimler and Karl (who later changed his name to Carl) Benz, whose companies merged in 1926, believed in competition as a means of proving the worth of their creations. The Paris-Bordeaux-Paris race of 1895, the first automobile race ever held, saw two Benz creations compete, finishing in fifth and thirteenth places. On Thanksgiving Day of that year, the first American competition, the Chicago Times-Herald race, also had two Benzes entered.

A Mercedes
racer from
1914. The
company's
output from
1910–19 was
outfitted with
Knight sleeve-
valve engines.

In 1899 Emil Jellinek, who would go on to be a Daimler distributor, bought a 28-horsepower, four-cylinder vehicle and used it to compete that year in the Nice Week races. Baron Arthur de Rothschild bought the car when it proved faster than his own. Jellinek in 1900 offered to order three dozen 35-horsepower Daimlers if the company made him its exclusive agent for Austria-Hungary, Belgium, France, and the United States. He also had one other condition: being a proud papa, the cars were to be named after his daughter, Mercedes. Daimler agreed, and Jellinek raced the new car during Nice Week 1901, where it reportedly dominated events.

For ten years prior to the start of the First World War, all automobiles from Benz & Cie were powered by four-cylinder engines, had chain drives, and were designed for competition. Horsepower (hp) output climbed steadily, from 60 in 1903 to 120 by 1908. The company's final chain-drive car was the most famous, the "Blitzen Benz," in which American daredevil Barney Oldfield captured the world land speed record in 1910, exceeding 131 miles per hour (210kph).

This 1927 S-model Gangloff tourer illustrates how coach-builders could develop very rakish designs on the drop-center frame.

Mercedes, meanwhile, outfitted its cars from 1910 to 1919 with the Knight sleeve-valve engine, with one such vehicle achieving a fifth-place finish in the 1912 Indianapolis 500, the second running of the classic race.

After the two companies merged, their developmental efforts paralleled the fever for grand prix racing that was then sweeping Europe. Launched in 1926, the type "K" (for *kurz*, German for "short") model had a 133.9-inch wheelbase and a supercharged 6.2-liter six-cylinder engine good for 140 hp. Race driver Rudolf Caracciola started his legend of invincibility in Mercedes-Benz cars that year by winning six events with one.

Concurrent in development with the K were the type "S" (for sports) and SS models. Built on a drop-center frame, the new design had the radiator and engine moved a foot toward the rear of the car, which lowered the center of gravity and did wonders for handling, while encouraging the custom coach-builders of the era to outfit the cars with their most rakish designs. These efforts from the 1930s are today regarded as legitimate works of art in the field and many feel them to be the most stunning motorcars ever created.

It wasn't until after the Second World War that Daimler-Benz made its greatest claim to the sporting tradition. Its factories rebuilt with Marshall Plan dollars, the company decided that its competitive efforts would focus on sports car racing rather than grand prix efforts. A 3.0-liter, six-cylinder engine was fitted into a newly designed tubular space frame and a slippery body was developed, one that generated a drag coefficient of only 0.29 cd.

Launched in 1952, the 300SLR racing saloon lost only one race during its fabled career, creating considerable demand for the production variant that followed.

This street car, the 300SL, was known informally as the Gullwing Coupe, as the tubular space frame prohibited the use of conventional doors. This feature was revised in the Roadster variant, which first appeared in 1957, a car the company promoted as having outstanding road performance, plus luxury. Chrome trim and a leather interior complemented its classic sports car lines, setting a tone for the company's two-passenger sports cars that followed: the 230SL, 250SL, 350SL, 450SL, to the SL500 and SLK230 offered today.

Many of the company's four-passenger cars—the cabriolets and two-door coupes—have also boasted through the years a panache that tickles the fancy of enthusiasts. Daimler-Benz, ever mindful of the need to repay its Marshall Plan factory development loans, diversified its platforms to appeal to a broad range of tastes. Its coupes and top-down four-seaters offered a certain component of fun, yet they also provided a stately means of transport, a combination of virtues that to this day remains distinctly Mercedes-Benz's own.

Even Mercedes' stoic four-door sedans have occasionally been recognized by their customers for their value in competitive efforts, if for no other reason than that they are solidly built. The company had several rally successes with S-class saloons during the 1950s and '60s; in more recent times they've fought nobly in European "Touring Car" class road races, chalking up several wins.

Thus have the distinguished cars of Mercedes-Benz put a gleam in the eye of the driving enthusiast over many decades.

FOLLOWING PAGE: Production 300SLs varied little from the original 1952 competition coupes. They had no air conditioning and minimal ventilation, but they looked cool in another sense of the word.

Pictured at the National Motor Museum
in Beaulieu, England is this replica of
Carl Benz' first car, the Patent-Motorwagen.

CHAPTER ONE

Birth and Rebirth

Mercedes-Benz motorcars, in today's culture, represent luxury, security, and technological refinement. The secure place this icon holds in our collective history, however, reflects a corporate history that has been threatened with extinction more than once.

To begin with, two separate companies had to agree to a merger. Both entities were namesakes.

From the doors of a Mannheim workshop in 1885 emerged a three-wheeled contraption powered by an internal combustion engine. In its seat was Carl Benz, an engine designer, who had assembled a crew of bicycle mechanics and other innovators to create the device. It won a patent from the German government on January 29, 1886, and the Patent-Motorwagen is recognized today as being the first automobile.

Meanwhile, in the town of Cannstatt, 60 miles (96km) away, Gottlieb Daimler had himself received a patent for an internal combustion engine, which a colleague, Wilhelm Maybach, was using for a four-wheeled self-propelled carriage known as the Daimler Motorenwagen.

Within five years, both Benz and Daimler were involved in the production of motorcars, a product at the time that not many were clamoring for. Unfazed, Benz diversified his line to include the Viktoria and Velo models, and then, in 1898, the Ideal.

Elegant in their own way, these early Benz models essentially were simple motorized buggies, or, in the vernacular of the time, *voitures.*

Early Benz motorcars, such as this 1900 model, were really no more than motorized buggies, known at the time as "voitures."

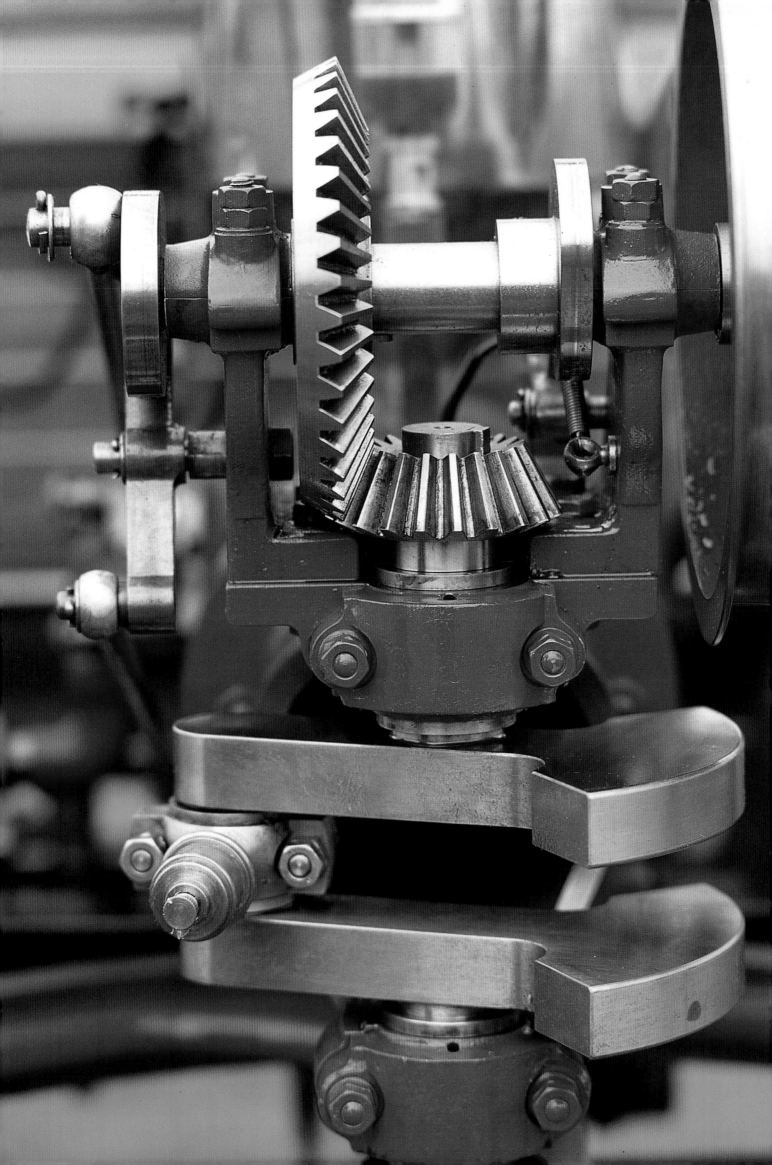

Meanwhile, Daimler was busy exploring every conceivable application that could possibly use an internal combustion engine—on land, in the air, or on the water—which is why his company, Daimler Motoren Gesellschaft, created a three-pointed star as its emblem. Daimler himself died in March of 1890, and the vision of his company ended up in the hands of Emil Jellinek, who distributed Daimler automobiles throughout Austria-Hungary, France, and Belgium.

Jellinek believed the public would embrace the automobile if it could be made faster and more stylish, but Daimler's conservative board members didn't see things that way. An appropriate design had been penned by Paul Daimler, son of the founder, but the board hadn't given it the green light for production. To bring leverage to the new concept, Jellinek proposed buying the first thirty-six vehicles produced, but he did impose a unique condition: that they be named after his daughter, Mercedes. The board capitulated, and what resulted was the first modern automobile. It had the engine in the front, a radiator in front of the engine, four wheels, and was built on a frame of steel instead of wood.

These first Mercedes automobiles were hard to beat for innovation in design and performance. At the time the Mercedes 40 hp model boasted the most powerful engine one could buy in 1902, and offered innovations such as water-cooled rear brakes, a honeycomb radiator, and a four-speed transmission.

The Patent-Motorwagen's internal combustion engine was started by spinning its weighted flywheel.

Gearing between the Patent-Motorwagen's flywheel and drive pulley shows the high degree of craftsmanship exercised by Benz' crew of bicycle mechanics in creating what is regarded as the very first automobile.

A 1912 Mercedes 37/90, the Prince Henry Torpedo, nicely illustrates the chain-drive mechanism that was typical of Mercedes motorcars of the period.

Offerings from competitors paled in comparison, and this was no different for Benz & Cie. Sales fell, and Carl left the company to his sons, Richard and Eugen, who went to work creating a more modern vehicle. This became the Parsifal of 1903, and with its vertical, two-cylinder engine and shaft drive, it was intended to provide direct competition for the Mercedes. Build quality was suspect, however; Richard and Eugen left, and Carl returned to the company. For the next ten years, all automobiles from Benz & Cie were powered by four-cylinder engines, had chain drives, and were designed for competition. The company's final chain-drive car, the "Blitzen Benz," proved to be its best known, following Barney Oldfield's 1910 record run.

Mercedes, meanwhile, would outfit its cars from 1910 to 1919 with the Knight sleeve-valve engine.

*The 1903 Mercedes was considered the
first modern automobile, with its engine
in the front, a radiator in front of the
engine, four wheels and steel frame.*

Perhaps one reason for the overt stylishness of the 1911 Benz Labourdette skiff was the fact that it made for American hatmaker William Stetson.

Benz motorcars were essentially conservative designs—until custom coachbuilders worked their magic. This 1911 90 hp chassis features a wooden "skiff" body designed by Henri Labourdette.

A 1908 Mercedes touring car. These early designs set the standard in the nascent automotive world for design and performance.

*The 1922 Targa Florio
race car was emblematic
of Mercedes' technical innovation. It boasted a large,
steel, channel-section frame,
and its wire wheels rode
on semi-elliptical springs.*

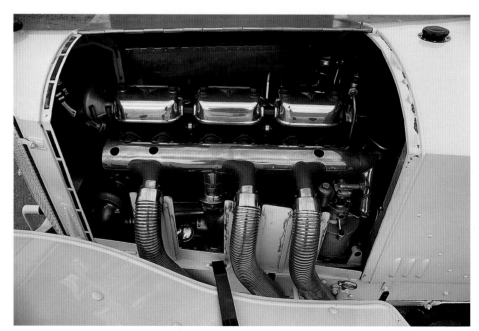

*The Targa Florio was powered
by an overhead-cam, six-cylinder, inline engine that powered
the car through a clutch made
of double leather cones, mated
to a four-speed transmission.*

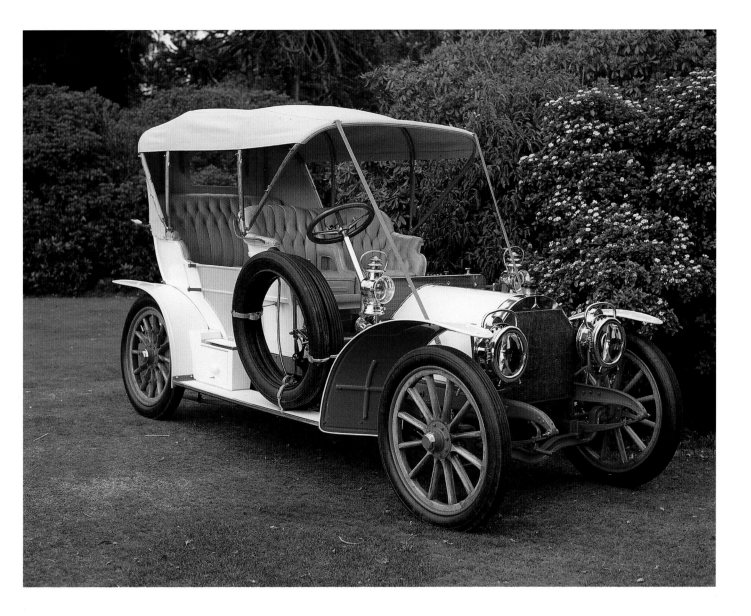

The American Market Beckons

Such efforts created a growing interest in German cars in the American marketplace. Since 1888, piano maker William Steinway of Long Island City, New York, had been a Daimler agent, envisioning a great future for the company's engines in boats, buses, and trolleys. The popularity of the Mercedes, however, led Steinway to obtain a manufacturing license, and from 1905 through 1907 his Daimler Manufacturing Co. built American Mercedes automobiles. Such offerings, being built by hand and furnished with often-opulent coachwork, cost up to four times as much as the mass-produced auto-mobiles sold by American carmakers Raymond Olds and Henry Ford.

Both Benz and Mercedes were building the most impressive cars of the era. Emblematic of Mercedes' technical innovation was a competition car from 1922 called the Targa Florio, named after the Italian road race in which it was entered. It had a large, channel-section frame made of steel, and its wire wheels rode on semi-elliptical springs. Its six-cylinder, overhead-cam, inline engine powered the rear wheels through a clutch made of double leather

Altogether lovely is this 1904 Mercedes 28/32 Double Phaeton, despite its missing windscreen. Similar cars were built under license in the U.S. from 1905–07 by the Daimler Manufacturing Co., Long Island City, New York, owned by piano manufacturer William Steinway.

cones, mated to a four-speed transmission. The mechanicals also served as the foundation for the Type 630 Mercedes 24/100 series of production cars that Paul Daimler had designed.

Fine machines these were, but the fact was that expensive automobiles had not caught on with the German public at large, particularly one dealing with an inflationary postwar economy. Daimler-Motoren-Gesellschaft and Benz & Cie therefore commenced talks in 1923 about possibly merging their operations. In May of the following year, the two firms signed a noncompetitive agreement that saw their separate service, sales, and promotions departments consolidated; an agreement to merge came in 1925. Finally, on June 28, 1926, the new company, Daimler-Benz Aktiengesellschaft, was formed.

The company initially promoted and sold existing designs—the Stuttgart and the Mannheim, named after the respective bases of operation of the old firms. These were somewhat ordinary efforts, and at the outset Daimler-Benz received far more notice for its immediate success in competition. The first Grand Prix of Germany was held in 1926, and it was won by a Mercedes-Benz, driven by the legendary Rudolf Caracciola. He went on to become a regular factory driver, and thus was born a fabulous racing history, as Caracciola and cars bearing the three-pointed star chalked up win after win in the years leading up to the Second World War.

The front view of this 1929 SSK nicely shows the bent front axle that is part of its "drop-center" frame, a design that lowered the car's center of gravity and greatly improved handling.

*The office of the
1929 SSK, although
spartan in features,
was richly finished
with walnut and leather.*

The company's first new car was the Model K of 1926. Chief engineer Dr.
Ferdinand Porsche had started with the 147.5-inch wheelbase chassis of Paul
Daimler's Type 630 and then reduced it to 133.9 inches. Its 6.2-liter engine
was fitted with a Roots supercharger, which boosted its output from 100 hp
to 140 hp when engaged. It could reach a straight-line speed of 90 mph
(144kph) and was the fastest production vehicle in the world at the time.

Simultaneously, a racing variant was developed, the S, for the sports model.
It had a narrow body and was built on a new drop-center frame that encour-
aged private buyers to invest in quite rakish coachwork; but the S's narrow
line limited the creativity of aftermarket designers, and this led to the development of the SS, and ultimately the SSK, which by 1929 was producing
250 hp when supercharged. Wider, and with a higher bodyline, the SS series
allowed coachbuilders such as Van Den Plas of Brussels and Soutchik of
France to create memorable saloons, touring cars, and cabriolets.

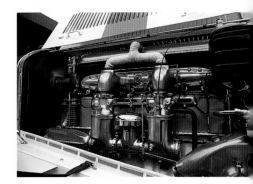

*The SSK benefitted
from a Roots super-
charger that, when
engaged, boosted out-
put from the 180-hp
inline six to 250 hp.*

The Boattail Speedster

Perhaps the most evocative specimen of this series was bodied outside
of the continent. In 1928 Howard Isham of Santa Barbara, California,
commissioned the Walter M. Murphy Co. of Pasadena (known for its work
on Dusenbergs) to create a convertible on an SSK chassis that had a sloping
windshield and a tapered rear end; it was dubbed the Boattail Speedster.
Its hood was enormously long, its fenders swooped, and it was perhaps
the raciest-looking automobile on the planet in the year before the Great
Depression hit.

As a merged company, Daimler-Benz initially focussed on existing designs, such as this traditional 1926 Mercedes Stuttgart 200.

Nineteen twenty-eight was also the year Daimler-Benz introduced its new Nurburg 460 model. Powered by a 4.6-liter inline eight-cylinder engine, it had an overall length of 16 feet, 3 inches (4.95m). The car got its name from the Nurburgring racing circuit, where a prototype had averaged more than 40 mph (64kph) over a then-record thirteen-day, nonstop endurance run. Nearly 2,900 460s were produced by the time production ceased in 1933; they were bodied usually as open tourers, limousines, or cabriolets, although a special sports-roadster version was also available.

The company's next efforts with eight-cylinder cars resulted in some truly majestic creations: the 500K and 540K series. Many consider these to be among the most beautiful works of automotive art ever assembled.

Their chassis design was first seen in 1933 in the Type 380, but its 3.8-liter inline eight wasn't really up to the task of propelling the 5,000-pound (2270kg) car. The following year the engine was replaced with a 5.0-liter straight eight, and a legend was born.

FOLLOWING PAGE:
*A 1929 Mercedes-Benz
SSK, thanks to its super-
charged, 6.8-liter, inline
six, could reach the magi-
cal top speed of 100 mph.*

*A close look at the front
of this 1936 500K Special
Roadster offers a view of one
of the most complex radiator
designs of all time. Each
opening represents a single,
individually soldered tube.*

*This 1936 500K Special Roadster, long and sleek on its 129.5-inch
wheelbase chassis, offered quality, comfort and considerable style.*

Another '36 500K Special Roadster. Exhaust pipes were contained within polished, flexible heat shields, a design hallmark for the car.

Handling and comfort was the hallmark of the 500K and 540K series, thanks to a four-wheel independent suspension system designed by Dr. Hans Nibel and Fritz Nallinger. The rear suspension consisted of a swing axle with two huge coil springs at each wheel; in front each wheel had parallel wishbones, mounted on rubber bushings to deaden road shock, and a single coil spring. The design allowed the front wheels to flex slightly to the rear, as well as vertically, on impact with a bump, softening vibrations even further.

Wilhelm Maybach's four-speed manual transmission design was utilized to harness the engine's output, which was considerable; in top gear, the 500K could exceed 100 mph (160kph), legendary speed at the time. In 1936, a 5.4-liter engine was fitted, and the design was in full flower. Capable of 115 hp unblown, and 180 hp with the supercharger engaged, the 540K was one of the most powerful production automobiles one could buy in 1936, yet as *Motor Sport* magazine stated at the time, it was capable of "a gliding crawl in absolute silence."

Although the chassis was designed to be fully exploited by coachbuilders, almost all of the dozen-plus body types fitted to the 500K and 540K were produced by the company at Sindelfingen. Saloons, limousines, "Kombinations" (a convertible coupe with an optional removable hard top), the Sport-Roadster, the Spezial-Roadster (which had a divided "V" windshield and a metal cover for its concealable top), phaetons, and five different cabriolets were offered. In all, 354 500K chassis were built from 1934 to 1936, while 406 540K chassis were produced from 1936 to 1940.

The 540K designation was formally applied somewhat after the fact, as thirteen of the 500K chassis ordered during late 1935 were fitted with the 5.4-liter engine. Only three of these thirteen cars still exist. One particularly beautiful example is a 1935 540K Cabriolet A, owned by Frank Cherry. In red, with a saddle leather interior and a black cabriolet top, it is a significant demonstration of how the series combined personal sportiness with elegance.

As far as the company was concerned, the 540K Special Roadster, introduced at the 1936 Berlin Auto Show, was its ultimate creation. The most expensive Mercedes-Benz offered to date, it was a massive automobile. Two could be seated in the cockpit, and another daring couple could ride in its rumble seat. Its convertible top could be made to disappear beneath a metal lid. Chrome was everywhere, trimming the fenders, the long hood, the doors, and massive combination spotlights/rear-view mirrors found on both sides of the split-V windshield. Each of the chrome fittings was made from a special casting. Fine leather upholstered the interior, and the gauges in the dashboard were surrounded by a mother-of-pearl inlay. The steering wheel and control handles were all white. In terms of sheer styling, the Special Roadster was uncompromising.

The ivory shift knob and steering wheel, here in a 500K Special Roadster, would become signature items in other Mercedes-Benz touring cars in ensuing years.

A 1938 540K Cabriolet. The top, when lowered, created a stack of fabric, bows, and headliner that obscured the view to the rear.

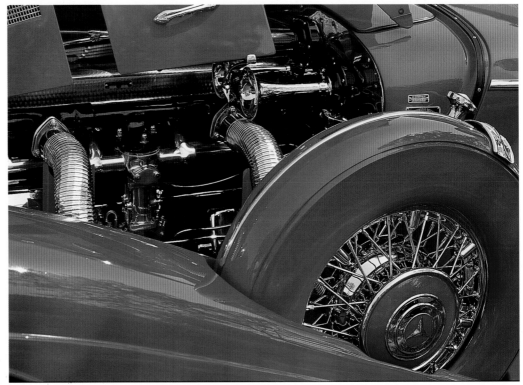

The 540K was powered by a 5.4-liter engine that produced 180 hp when supercharged. The car was produced through early 1940.

Prosaic, Yet Still Elegant

Of course, such expensive products as the 500K and 540K could not on their own sustain the company. Its success was tied more to the 290, 230, and 170 series.

With its boxed drop-section chassis, four-wheel independent suspension, overdrive transmission, divided track-rod steering, and one-shot lubrication system, the 68-hp 290 incorporated advanced thinking when it bowed in 1933. Utilizing an inline six-cylinder engine, most of the 8,214 290s built through 1937 were assembled at the Mannheim Werke and had conventional styling.

A few 290s, particularly the Streamlined Saloon, Roadster, and Cabriolet, were bodied at Sindelfingen and, in luxury trim, were embraced by the public as more affordable versions of the 540K, as they listed at exactly half the price. The 55-hp Type 230, even more affordable, was also a platform for some elegant body work, particularly in the Cabriolet A variant produced between 1936 and 1937.

Mercedes-Benz's best-selling car of the 1930s was the Type 170. A mass-market car introduced in 1931 to help European buyers weather the Great Depression, it was a conservative design but still relatively innovative compared to other continental offerings. It had a 1.7-liter six-cylinder engine, along with four-wheel independent suspension, four-wheel hydraulic brakes, and an antitheft lock on the steering wheel.

In terms of appearance, the squared-off 170 was a bit of an ugly duckling compared to its upmarket siblings. But in 1936, the 170V was introduced. Its tubular backbone frame helped improve ride quality, and its new 1.7-liter four-cylinder engine, at 38 hp, offered more zip. As a two-seat roadster, the 170V provided a very satisfactory, sporty motoring experience, accessible to anyone who had $1,250 to spend in 1938.

Nearly 100,000 variants of the 170V, in ten different body styles, were produced between 1936 and 1942, when the war mandated that domestic automobile production be replaced by aircraft engine manufacturing. The war nearly destroyed the company, but the plucky little 170V would ultimately save it.

A 1937 540K Special Roadster, one of the most stunning automobiles ever created. Some consider the lines arrogant.

During the 1930s, Mercedes-Benz dominated Grand Prix racing. This 1938 W165 shows the bare aluminum skin that inspired the name of the factory race team: the Silver Arrows.

The Mercedes race team received considerable support from the German government during the 1930s, allowing team engineers to create complicated jewels such as this 1.5-liter engine in the W165 racing car.

This 1937 230 Saloon was an intermediate model, powered by a six-cylinder engine that produced 55 hp.

A 1952 variant of the plucky little 170V Saloon, the car that provided the foundation for Mercedes-Benz' postwar resurrection.

CHAPTER TWO

A New Sporting Tradition

Daimler-Benz had paid a huge price for its participation in the Nazi war effort, as its Board of Directors acknowledged in a December 1945 memorandum, stating that by this date the company had basically ceased to exist. The Sindelfingen plant, for example, had been 85 percent destroyed.

The good news was that there was incredible market demand for product in the years immediately following the war. It was estimated that in 1945 the German sectors controlled by the British, French, and Americans (what would come to be known as West Germany) urgently needed 25,000 cars, 10,000 motorcycles, 9,000 trucks, and 5,000 buses. Top priority was given to vehicles that facilitated trade, and by the end of the year the Mannheim plant, which had largely escaped bombing, was in business producing three- and five-ton trucks.

Other good news included the fact that Allied bombs had somehow missed most of the production tooling for the 170V saloon. By June 1946 its chassis was being used to make pickup trucks, delivery vans, and ambulances.

Politics played its role in the postwar revival of Daimler-Benz. A new, stable deutsche mark was issued in 1948, replacing the now worthless reichsmark. Nineteen forty-eight was also the year the Marshall Plan started to bring economic aid to western Europe; eventually West Germany received $3.5 billion in funding for reconstruction. The company renovated its factories, making Sindelfingen the focal point for auto construction, with other factories focusing on engines, trucks, and buses.

Production began on evolutions of prewar designs. In March 1949 the 170S bowed, an upmarket version of the 170V with coil front springs and an alloy cylinder head. They were joined in May 1949 by the 170D, a diesel-engined version of the 170V. In the fuel-starved postwar years, the economy offered by a diesel engine made sense to German consumers, and they bought swarms of the cars, making it the best-selling Mercedes-Benz of the time.

The 170D was also significant in a technical way, as the engine had pushrod-actuated overhead valves, instead of side valves—the first Mercedes-Benz to do so.

It wasn't until 1951 that performance began to return to the Mercedes-Benz marque. The 220 that was introduced at the Frankfurt Motor Show in April 1951 was essentially a 170S on the surface with modern, flush-fitting headlights, but it was powered by a new six-cylinder engine, the M180, designed for high performance. Large-diameter valves and a short piston stroke allowed the engine to breathe well at high revs, and the overhead camshaft was now chain-driven instead of pushrod-activated.

The M186 3.0-liter engine that powered the prestigious 300 series which bowed a few months later was also innovative. This larger engine was designed for smooth power delivery, so it had a long cylinder stroke that did not rev quite as freely, and seven main bearings, instead of the four found in the M180 engine. Like its little brother, it had an alloy cylinder head and a cast-iron block, but it dispensed with conventional carburation in favor of a mechanical direct fuel injection system, the first use of this technology in a mass-produced, gasoline-powered car.

The model series that the M186 powered had an extraordinarily successful eleven-year production run. The first 300 sedan was built in late 1951. With four doors and slim pillars, it was a stately vehicle often used for transporting dignitaries and government officials. For those a tad more frivolous, a four-door convertible entered production in April 1952.

In early 1954, a successor, the 300b, was introduced. The body was the same, but the car received refinements in the form of front vent windows, larger brakes, and 10 more horsepower from the engine, now running a slightly higher compression of 7.5:1.

A hand-built variant, the 300SC, appeared late in 1955. It had a fuel-injected engine and a compression of 8.55:1, boosting horsepower to 175, along with larger brake drums. Comfort and performance were improved with a new independent rear suspension, which had a low-pivot-point rear axle with coil springs.

The 300SC was the most expensive Mercedes-Benz available at the time. It could be had as a roadster, coupe, or cabriolet. The interior featured plush, roll-and-pleat leather upholstery and finely finished walnut veneers, either straight-grain or burled. It also came complete with its own set of fitted leather luggage

A 1956 300S Convertible. Hugely expensive, it shared mechanicals with the 300 Saloon, and like it, was the last Mercedes-Benz to be built with a separate chassis.

The fuel-injected M198 engine used in the 300SL produced 240 hp, with the sports camshaft, when running at 5,800 rpm.

The Type 300 convertible used an overhead-cam, six-cylinder engine, and was one of the first truly modern postwar Mercedes-Benz creations.

Contemporary at Last

A truly new design, representing contemporary styling trends and manufacturing approaches, arrived in 1953 with the 180 sedan. Its unit-body construction and integrated, planar body surfaces seemed so radical to the Daimler-Benz board (remember, up to this point the company had produced cars with separate chassis and bodies) that it continued to offer the old 170 and 220 series, with their prewar lines, as a hedge should the new car prove unpopular.

This wasn't the case, and by 1954 a new six-cylinder car, the 220a, also featuring unit-body construction, bowed. The 220S (S for "super") followed two years later, and it wasn't long before the company used it as a foundation for more exclusive coupes and convertibles, which used a five-inch shorter wheelbase of 106.3 inches.

The 220S was initially powered by a 2.2-liter inline six fed by dual Solex carburetors, but by 1958 a fuel-injected version, the 220SE, was offered. New 220Sb "finback" sedans soon found their way onto the street, but the existing "round-body" 220SE coupe and convertible remained in production until the end of 1960.

In February 1961 the new 220SEb coupe was introduced, a handsome variant of the 220SE sedan. A sleek, trend-setting two-door that seated four in comfort, it was a worthy cross between a sports car and a touring sedan. Its fuel-injected, 134-hp overhead-cam six was mated to a floor-mounted, four-speed shifter. With the windows rolled down, there was no line at what would have been a "b" pillar position behind the doors, which contributed to a beautiful roofline and the gave the closed car quite an open feeling. This body style would last for a decade, providing the foundation for a larger-engined variant, the 1964 300SE coupe.

Custom luggage was an available option for the 220S Convertible of 1953, providing an added touch of luxury for which the company was famous.

The 1953 220S Convertible was powered by a new six-cylinder engine, the M180, that was designed for high performance.

An eye-to-eye view of the 300S Coupe. The 300 series was in production for eleven years, making it one of the longest-running models in Mercedes-Benz history.

The Sports Car Returns

During the early 1950s, Daimler-Benz had been thinking about returning to automobile racing, and the direction the company would take shaped the production of two-passenger production sports cars in all the years that followed.

Alfred Neubauer, who had headed the Grand Prix team to great successes before the war, was confronted in 1951 with the possibility that any development effort for a new open-wheeled grand prix formula car would be prohibitively expensive, as the sanctioning body planned to change existing formulas by the 1954 season in any event. Chief designer Dr. Fritz Nallinger then suggested that sports car racing might be an alternative, presuming a sports model could be developed from the 300 passenger sedan.

Rudolf Uhlenhaut, head of the research department, came up with the basic design for the car, which utilized a space frame of triangulated small-gauge steel tubing, very strong and very light in weight. The M186 engine was fitted with three carburetors and dual fuel pumps, a "trick" camshaft, and lightweight pistons, working at an 8.0:1 compression ratio. So configured, the engine was good for 175 horsepower. As for the body, Neubauer was influenced by attending the 24 Hours of LeMans in 1951, which the new C-Type Jaguar and its aerodynamic, Malcolm Sayer–designed body had won.

Uhlenhaut discussed his observations with Nallinger and Franz Roller, the company's chief designer, and they entrusted the project to Karl Wilfert, a designer in Sindelfingen. What Wilfert created was simply stunning. He chose a closed coupe body, which was felt would provide faster speeds on the seven-mile long Mulsanne straight at LeMans.

There was a quirk in the design, however. Because the space frame surrounded the sides of the cockpit, conventional doors could not be fitted. Mercedes engineers instead devised what would ultimately be known as "gullwing" doors, hinged at the roof's center, extending only as deep as the top of the fender line. When the doors were opened, they resembled the wings of a bird in flight.

Known as the 300SL (S for "sport"; L for *licht*, or "light"), the car was introduced to the press in March 1952 and three models competed in the Mille Miglia that May. Factory driver Karl Kling finished second in the thousand-mile tour, four-and-a-half

FOLLOWING PAGE
A 1953 300S Coupe had classically inspired, overtly sporting lines. Truly world class, it was one of the most expensive cars available at the time.

Although the trunk of the 1953 300S was steeply angled, fitting luggage was never a problem: each came with its own custom leather luggage set.

A 1955 300SL Gullwing coupe. Its sleek, rounded contours were a perfect match for its tubular space frame, with the hood, trunk lid, rocker panels, firewall, seat tub, and doors all made of aluminum.

*Mercedes-Benz intro-
duced the 300SL Road-
ster in 1957, replacing
the Gullwing coupe.
By 1964, 1,858 Roadsters
had been built.*

*The civilized interior
of the 300SL had leather
trim on the dashboard,
a two-tone instrument
panel, and a hinged
steering wheel to make
entry and exit easier.*

minutes behind Giovanni Bracco in a Ferrari, the first and last time the 300SL would be defeated.

The first win for the 300SL came at a sports car race in Berne, Switzerland, in late May 1952 with Kling driving. Notably, the great Rudolf Caracciola was driving a 300SL in fourth place when he lost control and hit a tree, breaking his leg. He spent the rest of the year in traction and then retired, his twenty-six-year career as a Mercedes-Benz driver at an end.

LeMans followed in mid-June of 1952. Four 300SLs were entered, with victory going to Hermann Lang and Fritz Reiss, followed by Theo Helfrich and Norbert Niedermeyer in second. The factory had achieved its goal in only a year, creating a new sports prototype from scratch and winning the most prestigious sports car race in the world.

Oddly enough, the company then decided to concentrate on grand prix racing after all, and withdrew from sports car racing until 1955. It did so with a sports car derived from the W196 grand prix car, the eight-cylinder 300SLR.

The car's success was phenomenal, winning the Mille Miglia (Sterling Moss drove, with journalist Denis Jenkinson navigating), the ADAC Eifel Race, the Swedish Grand Prix, the Tourist Trophy, and the Targa Florio, and ultimately the International Sports Car Championship for 1955.

The team could have won LeMans as well. Moss, driving a 300SLR roadster, had a twenty-minute lead in the fourth hour, when teammate Pierre Levegh innocently plowed into a pit straight collision between Mike Hawthorne's D-Type Jaguar and the Austin-Healey of Lance Macklin. Levegh's Mercedes launched into the air and into the crowd opposite the pits, bursting into white-hot flames fanned by its magnesium components. Levegh was killed, along with eighty-two spectators. More than a hundred were injured.

The team withdrew from the race out of respect for the dead, and, after the Targa victory, the Board of Directors sent Neubauer a letter stating that the company had decided, "after the most careful considerations, to withdraw from motor racing for several years." It would be more than three decades before the three-pointed star returned to the fray, but the memory of the wondrous car would be perpetuated in a commercial version, the 300SL Gullwing production coupe.

The Gullwing Takes Flight

The Gullwing originated after Max Hoffman, the American importer whose Frank Lloyd Wright–designed showroom was the pride of Park Avenue in New York, ordered one thousand 300SLs, giving impetus to two projects at once: an all-new sports coupe based on the platform frame used in the 180 sedan (which would ultimately become the 190SL), and the "civilization" of the 300SL racer for street use.

The latter effort ended up producing perhaps the most desirable of all post-war sports cars. It was fast, with the fuel-injected 3.0 six-cylinder engine now

A 300SL displays the gullwing doors that gave the car its nickname. Structural considerations for the tubular frame prevented the use of conventional doors.

*The Roadster's convertible top folded easily,
fitting beneath a flush metal cover that allowed
the car's lyrical lines to flow uninterrupted.*

*The new Roadster solved several problems of the Gullwing,
offering usable luggage space, superior handling, and
easier entry and exit through the use of conventional doors.*

A 190SL from 1956. A perfectly competent car in its own right, it remains somewhat unappreciated by collectors because it does not compare favorably with its big brother, the 300SL.

producing 215 hp, good for a top speed of 162 mph (259kph). It was beautiful, with distinctive "eyebrows" over the wheel wells and judicious applications of chrome, with more pronounced front fenders and a wider grill than those found on the racing coupe.

A great all-around sports car, the 300SL Gullwing was not an entirely successful production vehicle, as the doors, though modified, still made entry and exit a challenge, while the lack of roll-down windows made tollbooths particularly problematic.

These problems were successfully addressed when the 300SL roadster was introduced in 1955. The space frame was redesigned to allow for conventional doors. The chassis was stiffened to compensate for rigidity lost by the removal

of the roof, and the rear suspension was improved by the adoption of a
single-pivot swing axle design, while fatter tires and wider front and rear
tracks improved handling. A total of 1,858 roadsters were built before
production ceased in 1963.

Living in the shadow of the 300SL was the other offspring of Hoffman's
audacity: the 190SL. Styled to closely resemble its big brother, the 190SL,
with its four-cylinder, 1.9-liter engine, was a more affordable, purely "street"
machine. It appeared together with the first production 300SL on the stand
at the 1954 New York Auto Show, but brought a lot more money into the
company's coffers, with 25,000 examples being sold over its eight-year run.

A good car in its own right, it offered decent performance for a four-cylinder
car of the period, comparable to that of an Austin-Healey or a Triumph. But
its close resemblance to the race-bred 300SL brought performance compar-
isons it could not achieve, and Mercedes-Benz aficionados tend to look down
on the pretty little convertible as a result.

*As in the 300SL, a
huge speedometer
and tachometer domi-
nated the dashboard
of the 190SL. A four-
cylinder engine made
it an affordable alter-
native to the 300SL.*

*A 280SL, circa 1968.
Its 2.8-liter six was
good for 170 hp. By this
time the W113 design
was showing its age.*

The W113 Series

Two such differing approaches, as well as competition from the new Jaguar
XKE, caused Mercedes-Benz to rethink its sports car strategy in the early
1960s, believing there were customers who wanted something between
the extreme sportiness offered by the 300SL and the 190SL's touring car
ambiance. Both cars were replaced in 1963 by the first W113 platform, known
to consumers as the 230SL.

The company called the 230SL "the elegant car with the sporty character,"
and it would prove to be a popular car with women. Using the same floorpan
and engine found in the 220S sedan, the 230SL offered decent performance
and uncanny handling. It also had disk brakes in the front, an innovation at the
time. A three-speed automatic transmission was an option to the four-speed
manual gearbox.

The styling was unlike anything Mercedes-Benz had produced up to that
point. The little two-seater had appealing, yet decidedly rectangular lines, and

its headlights and turn signals were integrated into vertical assemblies. The widest grill ever seen on a Mercedes lay between the lights, sporting a large star medallion.

Its truly unique characteristic was the styling of the convertible's removable hardtop, which company designers referred to as a pagoda roof. Angular, with a large glass area for excellent visibility, the roofline was slightly raised at the side windows and depressed at the center, creating greater headroom for passengers, improved aerodynamics, and aided in the flow of rain off the car.

Three years later it was replaced by the 250SL, which was essentially the same car with a larger, 2.5-liter engine with seven bearings, a larger fuel tank, and larger, 14-by-6-inch (36x15cm) wheels. It lasted only fifteen months before it was replaced in turn by the 280SL and its new 2.8-liter, 170-hp six.

These W113-series cars were prized by their owners for comfort, reliability, and quality, but they were not the spectacular cars the 300SLs were. The design was becoming dated, and the company's sports car customers wondered what the future held in store. The much-publicized C111 test vehicle, created to allow the company to evaluate the Wankel rotary engine and capable of speeds up to 180 mph (288kph), whetted considerable interest but never made it out of the laboratory.

Many now wondered just how the company would integrate the future with its storied past.

The C111's cockpit. Only six of the 180-mph cars were built. A prominent American driver said he'd sell his soul for a chance to drive the car in a race.

The much publicized C111 test vehicle, introduced in 1969, gave Mercedes-Benz engineers a platform for testing Wankel three-chamber rotary engines.

In 1970 the C111 II made its appearance, differing only slightly from the original, thus teasing customers who wondered what future direction the company's sports cars wouldtake.

The engine in the 500SL was rated at 315 hp
and was good for an electronically limited
top speed in the United States of 155 mph.

CHAPTER THREE

Modern Classics

The 1970 model year got off to an auspicious start when Mercedes-Benz introduced its first coupes and convertibles to be powered by a V-8 engine. Both the 280SE 3.5 coupe and convertible were based on the body style used since 1961 in the 220SE, but they were powered by a new 3.5-liter V-8 that put out more than 1 horsepower (230 hp total) per cubic inch and could power the convertible to more than 130 mph (208kph).

The engine provided the foundation for a line of eight-cylinder engines that power Mercedes-Benz motorcars to this very day. The chassis was equally forward-looking—the fully independent suspension utilized coil springs at each wheel, as well as disk brakes. And the interior, completely lined in hand-selected and -fitted leathers, boasted a full range of luxury features. No other German car truly defined touring in style the way the 280SE 3.5 convertible did.

The new-generation SL sports car (whose platform received the factory designation of R107) bowed in June 1971, in the form of the 350SL. The pagoda roof was gone, but the car maintained the tradition of being a two-seated convertible with a removable hardtop. (An optional third seat allowed a passenger to sit sideways in the rear, but almost nobody bought it.)

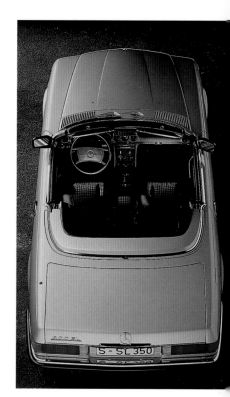

The 350SL, seen from above. When it was introduced in 1971, Road & Track magazine called it one of the "Ten Best Cars in the World."

Clean, understated elegance, as defined by a 1970 280SE 3.5 Coupe, one of the most handsome cars of the age.

The 220SE Coupe was considered a midrange luxury car, but it was far from austere. Judicious use of chrome and leather upholstery were decorative features.

A 350SL. These R107 SLs were the only cars to use lower bodyside moldings, which reduced body damage and stone chips, but were soon abandoned.

Even a car as stodgy as this 1982 300D sedan has handling characteristics to warm the heart of an enthusiast.

The company's entry level offering was the four-cylinder 190E sedan. A relatively small car, Mercedes-Benz purists spurned it, but it offered a level of luxury rarely found in compact cars.

A 450SLC hardtop. The V-8 SL line was first introduced in 1971, and remained in the product line through 1989.

By now new American regulations were causing automobile manufacturers to address environmental and safety concerns, and this led Mercedes-Benz to market the new SL as more of a safe, luxury vehicle rather an out-and-out sports car, and it had the features to back up these claims. It was fitted with wraparound turn signal indicators, breakaway outside mirrors, extra-strong "A" pillars, a slip-proof steering wheel, wide-sweep wipers, seat-anchored seat belts, pull-type safety handles, a recessed fuel tank, and self-cleaning, wraparound taillights. The instrument panel and steering wheel were padded (with leather, naturally). It weighed in excess of 3,400 pounds (1544kg), 300 pounds (136kg) more than the car it had replaced.

A 3.5-liter, dual-overhead-cam V-8 provided 200 hp for European-spec cars. Emission regulations for the American market demanded retarded spark plug advances, lean fuel mixtures, and low compression ratios, so to compensate for lost power Mercedes-Benz engineers increased the stroke of each cylinder by three-quarters of an inch (20mm), increasing engine displacement to 4.5 liters. America's initial 1971 models were thus badged 350SL 4.5; by the next year the car was officially rebadged as the 450SL. All American cars were fitted with three-speed automatic transmissions; European cars had standard four-speed manual shifters.

With its headlights rearranged in horizontal clusters, the overall shape of the car was that of a subtle wedge. Time had changed the character of the SL from a pure sports car to what *Sports Car World* called "essentially a two-door sedan."

Such understated ambiance leant itself to a strict hardtop version, the 450SLC, which was also created in 1971 by lengthening the chassis 4 inches (10cm), providing honest, albeit tight, accommodations in the rear for two additional passengers.

It would prove to be a fabulously successful touring car, even if enthusiasts tended to pass it by. The basic platform was in the product line for nearly two decades, through 1989. Mercedes-Benz addressed the car's initial lack of true sportiness by steadily increasing the displacement of the engine, so that by 1988 a 5.6-liter, all-alloy mill was powering the 560SL with 227 hp and 279 foot-pounds of torque. By the time R107 production ceased in August 1989, more than 237,000 units had been sold worldwide.

The midlevel Mercedes-Benz coupe of the 1980s was the 230CE, as exemplified by this 1983 model.

FOLLOWING PAGE: The R107 line was nearing the end of its run when this 1988 560SL first appeared. The 5.6-liter engine was the largest found in the series.

"Official" aftermarket variants of SL coupes have been produced by AMG, which offers tuning, handling and body refinements.

The 1980s also saw the company offer some interesting variations on the touring car front. One was the 1988 300TE, an update of the 300TD station wagon that Mercedes-Benz had offered for several years. The character of the wagon had been totally transformed when the venerable 3.0-liter turbodiesel of the 300TD was replaced by a 177-horsepower straight-six that ran on gasoline, the same engine the company was using in the 300SEL, 300CE, and 300E of the period. Stodginess in the family wagon was replaced by panache and dash.

Automobile enthusiasts during the eighties were also treated to some rousing modifications in S-Class Mercedes-Benz four-door sedans, performed by AMG, a German company that for years had been building and racing M-B sedans in European touring car competition. AMG was particularly known for its expertise in tuning engines and the re-engineering of Mercedes-Benz suspensions, and the factory chose to direct a few S-Class chassis to AMG before letting them loose on the market. Subtle, but virile, body modifications, such as air dams, rear spoilers, special fender flares, and rocker panels, as well as monochromatic paint schemes and special wheels, gave the AMG S-Class cars a muscular appearance to complement their outstanding performance.

The 300SEL was the quintessential Mercedes sedan of the 1970s. All American cars were autofitted with automatic transmissions.

A status statement that many Wall Street stockbrokers would come to love: the 1983 500SEC.

The 380SL was introduced in 1980 and was powered by a single overhead cam V-8 producing 155 hp.

The 1982 500SEC Coupe was powered by a 5.0-liter V-8; at the time it was the most expensive Mercedes-Benz one could buy— a perfect statement for the "go-go" 1980s.

This CE300 wagon looks ready to take whatever the road can dish out. Vehicle load-carrying is a major focus for the company, one of Europe's biggest makers of trucks.

Enter the R129

By now it was time to update the SL once again. Chief designer Bruno Sacco was charged with reinvigorating a platform that had grown bulky and lost some zip in its R107 phase. What his team came up with in the R129 was a radically new body and three new engines: a 3.0-liter six-cylinder unit (providing 190 hp with a single overhead cam, or 231 hp with dual cams), a 5.0-liter V-8 (dual cams, 326 hp), and, ultimately, a 6.0-liter V-12 (389 hp).

The multiple engine choices were a departure from previous generations of SLs, as was the choice for the top: a snug, waterproof soft top that retracted automatically at the touch of a button, disappearing under a metal lid. The top also featured a roll bar, controlled by sensors, that deployed automatically in only 0.3 seconds, much as air bags do.

The shape of the car was an aerodynamic wedge, and the body design featured trapezoidal headlights and an "A" pillar that totally integrated into the bodyline of the car. Behind the front wheel wells were air vents that recalled the original 300SL. The interior was an update of Mercedes-Benz's traditional combination of leather and wood trim; the dash featured easy-to-read white-on-black analog gauges.

Three models are available in the R129 series, reflecting multiple engine choice offerings— a first for SL cars.

One of the classiest means to get from point A to point B in 1986 was in the 300SL sedan. Stately, civil, powerful, yet nimble.

From 1989 through 1994, the cars were known as the 300SL and 500SL, depending on engine choice, but in 1995 model line designations were changed, with the "SL" now preceding the engine type. Nineteen ninety-six saw the six-cylinder car's displacement boosted to 3.2 liters, creating the SL320, a car that can reach 60 mph (96kph) in 8.8 seconds and has a top speed of 138 mph (221kph). The SL500 and SL600 have their top speeds electronically limited to 155 mph (248kph), at least in the United States.

Modern trapezoidal light groupings help define
the modern interpretation of the SL's grill.
Naturally, the three-pointed star badge is unchanged.

When it bowed in 1990, the 500SL reaffirmed the SL line's claim to being the ultimate in sporting automobiles. Still, it weighs more than two tons.

A 1992 "S"-class sedan. The company's flagship line offers engines ranging from a 3.2-liter V-8 through a six-liter V-12.

A 1992 600SL, with its V-12 engine and low profile tires, can startle with its performance, as well as with its $120,000 price.

Many bells and whistles are found on the SL600: anti-lock brakes, traction control, heated seats, and—oh yes— a cell phone.

The 6.0-liter V-12 found in today's SL600 generates 420 foot-pounds of torque and 389 horsepower, delivered through an electronically controlled five-speed automatic.

The car has proven a natural for the application of AMG's talents. AMG offered composite plastic/rubber body components for front and deck-lid spoilers, rear valence, and side skirts. Three-piece modular racing wheels—17 by 8 inches (43x20cm) in the front, 17 by 10 inches (43x25cm) in back—were fitted with low-profile Bridgestone radials. New rear differential gearing increased the final ratio from 2.65 to 3.27, and a sport exhaust system added an additional 8 hp. Buyers could also "trade in" the stock 5.0-liter engine for a stroked 6.0-liter variant good for 381 hp. A total package of such modifications would add as much as $45,000 to the 500SL's 1990 base price of $91,000.

Daimler-Benz itself proved capable of producing some pretty spiffy SL variants right out of the factory. For example, a limited edition of forty SL500s with a special Sport trim package of body pieces and wheels, and a lovely wooden steering wheel, was issued in 1996 to commemorate an inaugural running of the U.S. 500 at Michigan International Speedway. (The race sponsor was a cigarette manufacturer that had also sponsored a participating race team which powered its cars with Mercedes-Benz-badged engines, thus the tie-in.)

Today the ultimate SL is the 12-cylinder SL600. The 6.0-liter mill is the biggest ever in an SL, and generates 420 foot-pounds of torque with its 389 hp. The engine features inlet camshaft adjustment that improves volumetric efficiency in the cylinders, depending on torque requirements and engine speed. Power is put to the ground through an electronically controlled five-speed automatic transmission that has a backup hydraulic actuation system should the electronics fail. Working in tandem with the car's antilock braking and traction control systems, the gearbox improves traction by hastening or delaying shift points as conditions dictate. The car zooms to 60 mph (96kph) in less than six seconds, and lists for $125,000. Heated seats and a cell phone are standard.

Modern engine covers reveal little of the mystery beneath, but trust us, this AMG-tweaked 5.0 V-8 has galvanized giddyup.

AMG has extended its aftermarket offerings into the realm of finishes and interiors. The screaming chromium-yellow seats of this 500SL are definitely not standard.

The 500SL proved a natural for application of AMG's aftermarket talents, including plastic/rubber composite spoilers, valences, and side skirts.

A Question of Identity

What is the SL today, however? The designation originally meant "Super Light," which isn't really applicable for a two-ton automobile. For most motorists, today's SL is really a super touring car, best enjoyed with the top down, driven for no other reason than to enjoy a superlative motoring experience.

The recent Mercedes-Benz SLK is a different matter altogether. The nomenclature for this new roadster stands for *Sportlich, Licht, Kompact* (sporty, light, compact). When the first production model bowed at the Turin Motor Show in April 1996, it marked the first time that Mercedes-Benz offered two distinct sporting machines to the public since the days of the 300SL and 190SL forty years earlier.

Smaller, lighter, and less expensive than the SL line, the SLK230 is a true contemporary sports car design. Like the 190SL, the SLK is powered by a four-cylinder engine, this one a 2.3-liter, twin-cam, supercharged unit—the first production Mercedes-Benz to offer supercharging since prior to the Second World War)—good for 185 hp in its U.S. configuration (where it comes outfitted with a five-speed automatic transmission; elsewhere in the world a five-speed manual is standard).

Like the SL, the SLK has a fully automatic retracting top (the company calls these cars "coupe/roadsters"); unlike the SL, the top is hard rather than soft. Pushing a button lowers the car windows, unlocks the "Vario" roof, raises the trunk lid from special rear hinges, opens the roof, and raises a windscreen behind the roll bars. The roof folds, the trunk closes, and the windows roll up again, all in 25 seconds.

*FOLLOWING PAGE:
One of the design features of the prototype SLK that did not make it into production were the headrest fairings, otherwise the production version is remarkably similar to the prototype.*

The SLK230 is a relative bargain for a Mercedes-Benz, listing at just over $42,000. The automatic "Vario" roof takes only 25 seconds to retract.

When the prototype of the Mercedes-Benz SLK hit the auto salon circuit in 1994, it set the car-loving public abuzz.

Thanks to logic circuitry in its automatic transmission that adapts shift points to a driver's style, the SLK230 truly becomes an extension of the individual.

The SLK also comes with a carrier rack that can be used with or without the Vario top, increasing its appeal to a younger market that is fond of lugging sporting goods all over the place. Bright, two-toned interior treatments also add to the SLK's youthful appeal, as does its list price of just over $40,000.

A retrospective approach is used with the instruments, which are set in circular chrome bezels. The gauges have ivory faces, black numbers, and red needles. A carbon-fiber facing is found on the center console, around the air vents and the door handles.

The engine utilizes a thin-wall, cast-iron block, with an aluminum cylinder head for lightness, and is essentially the same engine used in contemporary Mercedes-Benz E-Class cars, modified for use with a supercharger. Four valves per cylinder allow for an 8.8:1 compression ratio. Engine management is by Motronic, with a single unit controlling fuel injection, ignition, anti-knock control, cruise control, and engine power for traction control, as well as an antitheft device.

The five-speed automatic is notable in that it features logic circuitry that, over time, "learns" the driving style of an individual and adapts the shifting pattern to fit. The result is an automobile that truly becomes an extension of the individual.

The SLK230 is the foundation of a contemporary product line that features performance throughout, more so than at any other time in Mercedes-Benz's 110-year history, even with the sedans. The contemporary C-Class sedan was introduced in 1994 and has become one of the company's most successful offerings. Today's C230 compares nicely with base offerings from competitor BMW and can be had for about $35,000.

The Mercedes-Benz SLK230 Kompressor is a true, modern sports car—one that boasts a fully automatic, retractable hard top.

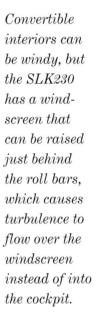

Convertible interiors can be windy, but the SLK230 has a windscreen that can be raised just behind the roll bars, which causes turbulence to flow over the windscreen instead of into the cockpit.

A 2.3-liter, twin-cam supercharged engine gives the SLK230 its heartbeat. A thin-wall, cast-iron block is topped with an aluminum head for lightness.

The 1996 E-Class Mercedes shown here is one of six models offered in this line. For those who can afford them, these cars are superb packages of styling and performance.

The company's most diversified product line is the E-Class line of luxury cars. Priced in the neighborhood of $45,000 to $50,000, they include the six-cylinder E300 diesel sedan, the six-cylinder E320 sedan, coupe, wagon, and cabriolet, and the eight-cylinder E430 sedan.

The flagship of the company remains the S-Class sedans, which today include two lengths of six-cylinder S320 cars, the eight-cylinder S420 and S500, and the mighty 12-cylinder S600. Two-door coupes, the CL500 and CL600, are also available; the latter, at $132,500, is the company's most expensive car that is generally available.

For those who believe that sportiness means the ability to cover all sorts of terrain, Mercedes-Benz now offers a sport utility vehicle, the ML320, for which at this writing a year-long waiting list has developed, just six months after its introduction.

There is one final Mercedes-Benz model available in Europe for customers demanding unlimited performance: the CLK-GTR, a barely civilized street version of an all-out, tube-framed, mid-engined racing car created for the FIA GT racing series. But even this 200-mph (320kph), fiberglass monster retains a traditional Mercedes-Benz grill, topped of course with a three-pointed star.

Yes, performance fairly percolates throughout today's Mercedes-Benz product line. At the approach of the new millennium, it seems more than likely that this philosophy, embraced by enthusiasts, will continue to be integrated into future product developments.

The CLK320 is an unusually sleek Mercedes-Benz coupe design. Now that the company has acquired Chrysler, could this be the shape of a future American stock car racing entry?

A 1996 E-Class sedan. The broadest range of Mercedes-Benz product offerings is found in this, its mid-sized line.

Built at its own plant in Alabama, the ML320 is the company's first sport-utility vehicle. A year-long waiting list instantly materialized upon its introduction.

The 12-cylinder SL600 coupe exudes purposefulness and performs accordingly. One would hope so, given the $125,000 price of admission.

Index